IN THE TALKING HOURS

Books by James Ragan

Poetry
In the Talking Hours
Womb-Weary
The Hunger Wall
Lusions
The World Shouldering I
Too Long a Solitude

Translations
Yevgeny Yevtushenko: Collected Poems (1952–1990)
(edited with Albert C. Todd)

Plays
The Landlord
Saints
Commedia

IN THE TALKING HOURS
POEMS BY
JAMES RAGAN

Los Angeles, 2004

IN THE TALKING HOURS
By JAMES RAGAN

Published by
FIGUEROA PRESS
Suite 401E
840 Childs Way
Los Angeles, CA 90089
Phone: (213) 740-3570
Fax: (213) 740-5203
www.figueroapress.com

Figueroa Press is a division of the USC University Bookstore

Copyright 1979, 2004 by James Ragan, all rights reserved

Cover, text and layout design by Jeff Ratto, USC GraphicDesign

Produced by Crestec Los Angeles, Inc.

Printed in the United States of America

Published in 1979 by Eden-Hall, 2000 by Herodias Books

Notice of Rights
All rights reserved. No part of this book may be reproduced or transmitted in any form or by any means, electronic, mechanical, photocopying, recording, or otherwise, without prior written permission from the author, care of Figueroa Press.

Notice of Liability
The information in this book is distributed on an "As is" basis, without warranty. While every precaution has been taken in the preparation of this book, neither the author nor Figueroa nor the USC University Bookstore shall have any liability to any person or entity with respect to any loss or damage caused or alleged to be caused directly or indirectly by any text contained in this book.

Figueroa Press and the USC University Bookstore are trademarks of the University of Southern California

Library of Congress Cataloguing-in-Publication Data
Ragan, James
In The Talking Hours
Includes no bibliographical references (p.) or index
ISBN: 1-932800-01-8
Library of Congress Number: 2004105386

for my Mother and Father

CONTENTS

The First Evolution: Fish and Wild Onions   11

I   ETHER ROOM

Insomnia: Gathering Bones	15
Eye Meditation for Insomniacs	16
On the Nature of Snoring	17
A Dead Twin Prays on the Eve of My Surgery	19
Bone-Step	21
Hammer	22
The Wounds	23
Gerasim	24
Losing a Sense of Balance	25
Ether Room	26
Tattoo: Your Dream the Night before a Birthday	27
Cacaphony	28
Bloom Falling Awake	29
Change of Season	30
Cancelling My Twenty-Sixth Year	32

II   DEATHWATCH

Prey and Predators	35
Aryan Devolution:	
For Eleven Israili Athletes in Munich	37
Fire Near Dead-Stream Road	41
To the Bronzed Mermaid on the Bowsprit of a Trawler,	
Aground Off Monomoy, Cape Cod	36
Sisyphus Blind	43
Archaeology in a Shoe	45

III   RECOVERY

Delivering My Brother, the Last Born	49
Prime Mate	50
Waiting for the Bus at Midnight	52
Defense Summation in the Trial of Hans Wilbur	54
Smoking Permitted to the Left	56
Her Fourth Ph.D. Discuss Party	57
Underground Wine Cellar, Athens, Greece	58
Backward Years	60

IV   IN THE TALKING HOURS

In the Talking Hours	65
Bringing a Stark Reality to the Screen	67
Dead Black Judy	68
Lombardo at Midnight, New Year's Eve, 1972	74
Just that Moment	76
Umbrella Man of Duquesne	78
Huckster at Noontime	80
To Pregnancy	83

V   THE SINGING HOUR

Junky Saints	87

IN THE TALKING HOURS

The First Evolution: Fish and Wild Onions

From birth we were curious
to pose as fish spawning out of accidents,
and suddenly a motion, fin on fin,
steadily upward into light.
And fearing it, we learned direction
by the lean odor of a camel's thigh.
We carried wind in the bag of our eyes.
With age we learned the currents,
to swim against the breath
of rocks, moss, the swift tongue
of a stream licking at our mouths.
We believed we were going forward.

At death we were promised ribs,
our photographs in shale.
In time the brain, a seed
in the pitch of our jowls.
Instead we hatched
as stalks for the wild onion.
Odors of light passed through our scales.
Breath rotted in our guts.
Each night in dreams we pulled out our roots,
peeled back the light. We wept
for creation, for the firstborn
of the fish, dead in our skulls.

It wasn't enough to cut through
the grain, to cry out of habit
or a lost skin. Instead we learned
to sleep backwards, returned
by yawns to our first inception.
We climbed from our beds
sideways like crabs
crawling back to sea, back into shade.
We prepared again
to predict our heritage, a third coming,
perhaps a man within us,
a seed, a shimmer of onion,
perhaps a fish swimming in shale.

I

ETHER ROOM

*Everything we do is decent when the mind
begins to forget—the design of life;*

Djuna Barnes
Nightwood

Insomnia: Gathering Bones

In beds I praise my genius.
I gather bones, toss them in the skull,
rattle them until they fall

out of place, connecting thumbs with legs,
arms with hips. At times a rib
bones its way into a palm

or rails the buttock
until I feel my fingers
split, half-way down each nail.

I even learn erogenous zones
of itching, somatic foreplay
to excite the bones, and maneuver feet

into position, toes above my head,
measuring balls into sockets,
fitting each into the other until they lock.

I rock back and forth,
insane with passing half my sleep awake.
In time the flesh will settle.

I will even feel the moon
beneath the sheets begin to rise sweating,
then fall, circling to caulk its usual space.

By morning I will gather all my limbs,
strap them to the brain, and sleepwalk like a horse
at a treadmill stepping wind around a stone.

Eye Meditation for Insomniacs

for a dead twin

Stare into a lightbulb, into its center
and think deeply about the rays
like fingers stuck in the corners of your eyes

or in the wall opposite you,
or in the shade at the back of the eyes,
watering as you squint, pretending sleep.

Keep the eyes free of lids or nose.
Look straight into the bulb
and let the light rock you.

You will see the Other Born Brother,
sleeping in a stocking,
quite dead by what a nurse calls

recovery, delivering an option.
And know by his fingers spread-eagle
along your nose, propping your lids,

he is surviving on your light, your sleep;
the bulb of his one eye stares you into blindness.
Now sleep with the blood of survival on your hands.

On the Nature of Snoring

> *I shall try and make a little creature*
> *to hold in my arms, a little creature*
> *in my image, no matter what I say.*
>
> Beckett, *Malone Dies*

I

Dead brother, twin-sleeper, bored
stiff in your rocking chair like a cartoon cat,
idling one-eyed stares at my bed,
you've tired of my snoring.

Sometimes I spy you on my fingernails,
undressing the cuticle's hard scraps
for shelter, clothes for an evening out
of wine, women, the lecher's itinerary—

or reading my fingerprints like pages,
fingering the scars for the sexy passage.
Your motives are simple. Necrophiliac,
masturbator of the senses, you rent corpses.
If caught, you'll escape identity.

II

All night you play the analyst, creature of habit,
the original *male fatale* reduced to prayer.
You meditate as if snoring were my life passing,
a slit tongue in the throat's dream of quiet,
a poem having nightmares.

Somehow I ignore your lack of notes,
the feedback on my stories.
Perhaps you've heard them all, Guru
of the yawn, the sneeze, the skipped heartbeat.
Now silence is your passion, your life-wish
to free this ghost of language,
my poet's stutter, Morse Code of monotony.

You'd rather take my pulse
like a priest hearing confession,
aroused only by the hesitations
in breath, the imagined story,
wet dream of the unknown,
paranoia,
mother god of invention.

A Dead Twin Prays on the Eve of My Surgery

I

He is possessed.
This need to talk all ourselves to death.
This prayer he conceives:
In the name of the father, the son,
and the Other Born.

Lecher
of divine insight, of fantasies
he creates in my dreams—
I've seen the way he looks at you,
undresses you in light, your image
safely drawn, in dark, behind his eye-patch.
He saves your photograph.

He is desperate.
This need to share my flesh.
Unborn twin, decomposed spirit
of a preternatural lust, he is jealous.
He sleeps with ghosts.
He borrows your name to dance this close.
He writhes his claws across my toes.
His sign is Cancer, home-body, voyeur to pain.
Already my foot swells,
takes its one false step. He moves in
to beget himself, to make things whole.

II

He has a bone to pick, revenge
on a father, now gone lame
with lust for offspring,
a guilt for misconceptions.
He would have us both disembodied,
specters, his trinity reduced to one.

Even now he wants you in his bed.
He would have me castrated,
the Amnesiac, crippled on this page,
to have this last dance,
to sing this poem,
to write me in your theology as his pen-name.

Bone-Step

Where my father lies, his pain late inside him,
where his body grows its extra weight, turning flesh
to waste, teeth to dice, one bone rattles closer to
    the kick.

Even now I test his grip to see the blood surge
    through
both our hands, rub the veins and know
his strength comes with exercise

of the mind, once centered in the bone-blood
of legs, arms, the heart within his heart.
It has moved out of thinking, out of skin-depth

into the marrow. We stand a bone-step away.
When we touch, we touch for the exercise and think
through gestures, step by step, our bodies into flesh.

Hammer

for my father

Even your eyes cave in
at the moment of waking
and breathe what follows sleep,

the tedium of light
through the inner eye,
still closed by the weight

of a hand rubbing
within, to get out, to stretch
along a thigh or breast.

If only you could dream
or think nails into a hinge
or stand straight

on this lathe rolling you
a thousand times past yourself
and see the difference

between standing in one place
and arriving. If only
you could pound

the hammer in your throat,
nail down the tongue,
talk silence to sleep.

The Wounds

Each night, father, before you died,
I climbed into your bed

where we stared
like victims, always at our scars,

massaged our eyes until the wounds appeared,
fresh, beginning their throb

beneath some bone
or fault in the flesh.

We had even cut our eyes
to know the colors

blood makes
and traced the taste down

along the lips to the tongue
and knew the wound

breath makes back along the throat
where we spoke, deaf, already blind.

Gerasim

for Ján Ragan (1901-1971)

Nothing was left to do
in your room spiced with ether,
but crutch my shoulders to your feet,
gloss the jute of skin
until the blood staled within their sacks.

In this room the candle
stinks of black crepe,
opium for pall-bearers,
lace to tie your shoes. You knew
the preparations, all the mirrors
I'd have to break
to lose your final face.

But still you pose, gums caulked with teeth,
deceive the mourners by your grave
indifference to a hand or lip
pressed against your veins, ignore
the sun strokes across your wreath.

I want your first face, gessoed
by the brush of light breaking through;
your eyes in motion, bones colliding,
your body flowing, painted to the toes.
I want a portrait in this gallery
where only still-lifes hang.

Losing a Sense of Balance

It comes with the weather,
wet grass on the ball of my foot,
limping, kicking off the sun
to keep my flesh smooth, free

of roots, of growing
too much to bear.

It comes with cutting hair,
the weight of my forehead
pulling the ears, out-
growing the rest of me

with brains, with thinking
stones breathe, live forever.

And sometimes with losing a woman,
a bone of me,
dying,
gone.

Ether Room

I awake within your breathing,
catching my breath;
it belongs to you for a moment,
rehearsed in voices,
by art, by habit.

I learn my legs,
how to lose all sense of lift or fall,
to hang by my toes
from a rope, spinning
while all your voices scream

then stop
too soon to collect your body catching up;
it arrives long after my own
body heals, stands
still, caught up in its beginning
flesh and odor.

I try to breathe through
gauze, through the cure,
and feel the collision, flesh against bone,
the mind's falling out,
the anonymity of nose
cutting windshield like diamond,

and know finally
what it means to lose a face,
your face, arranged in sheets, white
like ether rolling around my eyes
to hold you still, at your center,
while all the other dark
                    bone forms
   spin, slip by.

Tattoo:
Your Dream the Night Before a Birthday

You insist the colors are not important
nor the background, flesh
pocked where you tried to burn
a way out of yourself. Instead
you praise the needlework,
its webbing spanned across each breast,
and reflect on how you warmed the slab,
how your torturer stretched you
inside-out, to prick the thews,
to get to where the blood thins,
to pin the wings to your ribs.
One butterfly. You forget
how long and deep into its flight
it carried you, spinning out
its weave in skin, in blood.
You remember only its eyes—
searching deeper and deeper for a death
in some dark part of you—
its flame, a chrysalis, and light.

Cacophony

Darkness wings out across your thighs
to touch my lap;
it breathes its sex inside me.
Its mouth has no ledge for jumping off.

I am bored with all this lovemaking.
Everything that falls
           falls into itself,
silence into silence; incest
between the touch and the thing touched.
Nothing is eased into flight.

Once I knew a blind man, full of talk,
whose walking stick had secrets
with the ground. It lured him in, face down,
where in the dark dust, drunk
                  he reared a woman,
ten children growing up.

I want to fall out of this body
of ourselves, out of flesh,
with an echo,
all the sound sucked in, drifting
until my mind cracks, inch by inch,
with the weight of my falling out.

Bloom Falling Awake

to Dyan

I search the bed again
down one side and up the other.
A white sheet hangs its cliff
before my eyes. The earth flaps.
Shadows underneath
give my fall a thousand bottoms
like echoes repeating landscape.
I retrace the steps back in;
a bed, the same white dream,
the sheet you drape across your thighs
to save your half of sanity. My half
gone, this fear of bed expanding,
space between us, this spinning,
on my axis, off high places,
this vertigo of mind's end.
I am falling off your body.
You call it suicide.
I call it survival
until the wind teaches me my wings
and I am meant to fly.

Change of Season

1

I wake
to another change of season,
to the wind and frost
nesting between the rafter's crotch,
to the shrikish claw of darkness
scratching shadows on the logs.

2

I sit
staring at suspended eaves,
at the corners of the walls,
the leaves that splash across the floor
seeking hands to touch,
at closets where starved wood rats
smear their leather lips
across the tongues of shoes,
at you,
drowned once again where dreams begin.

3

Outside,
the latticed shadow
plays possum cool among the trees.
It swings on branches across the water's mirror.
It scrapes shattered faces
from the river's bed
and shapes their reflections
like fingerprints along your face.

4

I chase
reflections like Cain,
lightning at my heels,
along retreating moonlight,
deep into the black nightshade,
into the blue flame of the lotus
where your face roots, flowers,
and is forgotten.

5

I walk
out of you,
shapeless like Abel's God,
into another dream
where seasons never change
and shadows are consumed
by a burning patch of sunlight,
loitering between the trees
like a starved woodsman hunting bear.

Cancelling My Twenty-sixth Year

Let's hope this year goes with all of you,
a lasting death, dark as flesh
to enter, loving still its waste,
the sperm that never rooted.

I could be many men at once,
changing wardrobes in my sleep
to lose a face, claiming hats are ties
to hang ahead on.

I would cancel years to study knives,
how the bone begets an edge at birth,
how my body dreams each night
to cut the rope, to fall

deeper into sleep. I have hung
myself in beds. Hats become my ledges.
Even now a knife carves your faces
in the moon. A rope roots in my head.

II

DEATHWATCH

and the day is fast approaching when nothing will remain but a fragment too tiny to hold.

Samuel Beckett
Malone Dies

Prey and Predators

I am lately looking back
at a stone hanging in the air,
testing its one last feather,

at sand flying wild
through the ribs of a bull
to sift free of the desert.

I suspect any stranger. In every room
there is something, someone stalking
the silent skip of my breath.

I have seen their smears
on a Tarot pack, their hands
on closed doors to a urinal.

They read palms off photographs
to determine days of rest.
Lifelines are their calendars.

When least expected they pretend
to be cousins matching blood
with old coins to settle a will.

They pay money at a garage sale.
At a slaughter house they eat bones
for a solid meal. A meat-hooker

once cornered them as worms
asleep within a statue's thigh.
Raw stone has become their bread.

Soothsayers of the writing wall,
they create the riddles, stones to solve the myths.
They would have me changing heads.

Even now in daylight I wish to be imagined
only as a necessary owl,
a light sleeper, victim of economy.

At night, avenger on a whole generation
of insomniacs possessed by my eyes,
by the death-drawl in the craw of my neck.

Aryan Devolution: For Eleven Israeli Athletes in Munich

I am Khepera in the morning.
I am Ra at noon.
I am Turn at eve.

B.C.

a.

The Olympians have long forgotten memories
of this Germany, this Munich, this stadium,
how they sat all day under threats
of half-moon, sickle and hammer,
hunched in their flags, athletes,
awaiting the sun's mad dash
like a hound down the track.
They expected Christ.
All the signs were there: September, Venus,
Magi in their slink suits
dragging dead camels toward the Star.

b.

Dateline—September 5, 1972
The torch cools at the rim of the stadium.
An odor of pitch-wax. Miles away
star-crossed saviors, kicking down the stretch,

stalk their trail of Jews across the Isar
to the city of knots. They are sorcerers.
They bale their prey like bines of grass.
In the square, dolls in stain-glass clocks
like old *muezzins* now drum,
dance away the hour.

    c.

A finish line.
In last wind sprinters lunge for the rope,
repeat the leap backward, now forward
for history, for the one-armed judge
\whose gun they jump
instinctively, off the starting block
where seconds lost are years of shoes
backtracking on their map of feet
to Sinai, to the desert strip of Gaza,
bones gathering like stars.

    A.D.

    b.

Black Septemberites,
forerunners of the fierce faith,
you predict our history:
the long-distance run of gods
to Mecca, Jerusalem, to prepare the stones,

the Wailing Wall and Kaaba.
You still promise us direction,
epiphanies of Ra turning to the East.

    a.

Magian prophets, who Lemuel banished to the desert,
stone-cutters, huggers of sand, planters
of the staked road West to Khartoum,
you still promise us the sun,
vanishing rock, Black Stone of destinations.
All around us stars are falling
in a dead heat. Only bones remain
chalked along the desertcourse.
Even now an astronaut falls to earth
with dust to grow a map.
He has promised us the moon.

    a.

A starting line.
It is the rock-maker's hour.
You are huddled around the stones
like vultures making camp.
You await the equinox, the *nativity
of the sun's walking stick*. The fires dim.
Prometheans are seeking oil for their lamps.

b.

Even the desert, once proud predator
of light, shivers under stones.
All night it shifts its past
the way a jackal with its prey
straddles water, sand, to hide its tracks.
A poet now recalls the *Nature Morte*,
the won and lost land of helpless power.
No one trusts your one-armed god behind his back.

c.

Postscript—Camp David, Sept. 17, 1978
Only spectators, we are patient with our flags.
We are running out of history.
We buy directions from our cabs.
Still we wait the next day and the next
for the sprinter running deserts with a torch.
He will never arrive. Nor the camels
who, for whatever dignity in death
came once to knot their tails in straw,
lie now, strangled at the Mosque,
wagging their tongues
for direction.

Fire Near Dead-Stream Road

Platte Lake, Michigan

We arrive with the long snow
on foot, our eyes the only light,
tracks of the last sled, our path
back to the road. Ahead

the clearing where we strike the match.
The wind stales the cold rush of smoke.
The river comes easy off the flame,
and for a moment, a fire
builds in our hands. We become inhabitants.

We would stay but the host
says fire near the road brings strangers in
to breed, to build the clearing up
into camps. A fire loses ground

to prophets, the usual ash and stone.
But we are civilized. We forge idols
out of wind. We shape footprints to survive us,
to freeze the river in where our bodies warmed
this altar, our eyes an offering, a last flame.

To the Bronzed Mermaid on the Bowsprit of a Trawler, Aground Off Monomoy, Cape Cod

Even the hunchback didn't know you,
hooking masts like gaffs into the Indian sky
and the look-out, high above the hawk's beak,
who watched you toss among the cuttlefish,
raped but still alive.
                Until I found you
dead where lovers go among the dunes,
your body lodged like driftwood,
breathing the moon's wet dust.
And their lust, how they rearranged the symbol
when you died: redeemer, virgin, saint,
all the monuments of birth.
                They were lovesick,
beachcombers with time to kill.
But I am all that dies, Ishmael
hugging the bowsprit where you hang,
afraid to spawn with the white-humped whale.
If only I could drag this sea
to find your mould,
                lie deep inside you,
braze your veins with blood, I would sleep
until your voice, whispering from the shoal
each time a wave fawns by, echoes
through my bones, through skeleton seamen,
tall, stiff-spined like spars grabbing wind-weight,
inching closer
                to a permanent death.

Sisyphus Blind

> *"A face that toils so close to stones*
> *is already stone itself."* —Camus

I have imagined him always blind,
pushing stone until the hill capsizes,
and the walk back down
becomes the walk back up,
each step, a shock, a touch of air,
on course in case a passer-by
leans into his world of local forms.

He stops. I barely brush his arms
before his eyes stare down,
calculating distance as I pass.
We are not far from breathing.
We suffocate only in the lungs
and curse each other, doubled-up, tongues
dried by the dust our shoe-flaps make.

Only night deceives us. Its landscape
trails the moon, shifting sky to cut us down
where we sit. We feel the shattering underfoot
of stars, the ground rolling overhead,
the rock carving paths into our flesh.
How willingly we fall into each other's cry.
We dream, eye to eye, one suicide.

I try to think his stare awake, to rise
above the ash of moonstone, to feel his shoes,
dust lifting around them. Nothing remains,
only rock, his moon-struck face.
I am whatever stone breathes, a blind man
pounding air to escape the universe
like a meteor burning up space.

Archaeology in a Shoe

1 *fossils*

Piecing inch by inch the soft
leather of the shoe, I learn its history:
fossils of a toe now extinct,
a nest of birds walking out
its sole, a hole where the man
climbed out, counted his years
by the ridges on the heel,
learned to kill birds and mice
for quilts, to survive the snow.
To survive the rat he grew nails,
shaped them into knives—
perhaps a case for genocide;
I'm still counting toes.

2 *extinction*

I want to survive myself.
I pull shoestrings from the old shoes.
I pump their lungs
like inner-tubes
to air-out odors of bird
wings, to revive the breath, my own
spirit in flight,
as if in spare tires I am promised
space to breathe my body in
to preserve the species;
as if in leather I am spared
inch by inch the long walk
around the toe of the man,
now extinct.

III

RECOVERY

*Dead World, airless, waterless.
That's it, reminisce.*

Samuel Beckett
Malone Dies

Delivering My Brother, the Last Born

> *He is learning, well behind his desperate eyes,*
> *the epistemology of loss, how to stand up*
> *knowing what every man must one day know*
> *and most know many days.*
> —John Berryman

They say in youth your head was battered
by a club, swinging at the wind of the ears.
Now you are deaf. In one ear a chord
strums for a dancing dog. In the other, silence
for the applause. You expect too much.

No game of bats and balls will bring you back
the soft wind beat of the drum you played
each time you kicked to breach your mother's skin.
Life begins with silence, not with a dialogue of feet.
Yours was a hard birth. It took years to free your
    skull.

Some say you teethed through the umbilical cord
and fell head-first into the slap of a hand.
Your face has been disfigured. Your ears still hum
in the wind. You are wearing braces for a tooth
whose only music is a dog tap-dancing on a drum.

Prime Mate

I'm this *primate*
they teach whores about—
Down on his luck
like a saw-tongued lizard, burrowing,
rolling ape on his spine
to throw the tail round full spin for the score.
Who hunches upright on his stalks,
half-moon and man,
balanced only by the weight of his genitals,
whose Lord's prayer lopes back and forth
in full orbit
as if from a string designed to strangle
or malign his hard progress.
Once the mandrake of an institution,
now Goliath, losing gravity,
walking three legs into ground
to root his tapered tail.

I've stood the curse for ages,
breasts hardly developed
for the Great War, liberation,
the sexless urge for unanimity.
The father milk has soured,
the skin rusted to a flat chest
from the leak, the holes
like dripping nostrils,
from years of beating *mea culpa* for a cave mate
or drooling over Davidia, her snake

body so much more advanced,
hair smooth to the waist,
breasts like armored plates,
hardly a fault from her prime
except for the break
at the crotch
and the tongue like a sling-shot.

This true prime mate,
who aims sadistically below the belt
to bring me down to one advantage,
of standing upright at the urinal,
ego-mania of concession—
I, the Lemur ape,
with that damned furry tail on backwards-
hardly an advantage at all.

Waiting for the Bus at Midnight

A lamppost of finger-streams,
the moon puffs a cloud
past ghosts of autumn, slips down
in a moment's cue and kicks
its muddy shoes and dusty bottom
dry of the night *serein*.

The act begins. A willow
sags to the steps, kneeling
where the town hall clock whispers
sermons to the monk, drunk
with Sunday talk. Crickets lying
in the mist settle to their pillows.

Only the car wakes, screaming
as the dog wags its tail
along the center stripe; bitterns
brag indifference to the star
and teenage lead, wearing slacks
too tight and dreaming

who sometimes, when she tiptoes
up to meet his tongue, stretches worlds
apart her buttocks, round, hypnotic.
She does not hear my breathing
but lips her lines so boldly
spinsters in bough-tressed windows,

like tramps, crippled by the cold,
see the smile, the rippled silhouette
of forms at rest, yet do not hear
his swoon stagger through the sweat
beneath her breast. I strain
to watch the drama hands unfold

and kiss her neck, its naked moles
like speckled dunes or shadows
stippled on the moon while he, flipping the coin
heads and tails, saddles the bench like Brando,
vacant, and overplays the role.

Defense Summation in the Trial
of Hans Wilbur

*A Park Avenue socialite filed suit in Superior Court,
charging a neighbor's dog with raping her cat.
Attorneys for Hans Wilbur, the accused canine, will
enter a formal plea of innocent by reason of insanity.*
—N.Y. Times, *January 1973*

I

Hans is not the ordinary dog,
the he-dog sporting leather paws,
dancing cat-calls in the cellar
where he spars the usual dark
barking back.

Instead he is neurotic,
walking shadows off through alleys, lawns,
urinating in shoes, afraid of trees,
teething weeds instead of bones,
always with a sense of guilt,
of being less than dog,
a eunuch dog,

a tragedy of youth
when once on pretense of learning back
ends of tails, three cats
saddled the hips to ride him bare,
reduced him to the boney dog
he is,

years of growing back the blood and hair,
still nauseous at the sound of cat,
the name of cat, maimed perhaps;
his left eye tilts
where the collar muzzled off
the ears.

Think of this dog,
condemned to rolling rubber balls,
rabid thoughts of bite
and limbs, of learning back
sides of flesh, a growing need
for skin.

II

We are on trial here
to think this dog sane
of malice, fleas, delusions of grandeur,
rubbing asses on the trees,
to think he might rape a cat, his bite
since gone,

as if by thinking
small in a big-ball town,
he could keep his wits about him,
grit his teeth, lick her tongue;
no doubt she teased him
into thinking bone.

Smoking Permitted to the Left

Please, no standing.
All things considered
in the back seat
where God plants us,
black tie, the unloosening
of your underthings
and the times I sweat
when the windows steam
at a drive-in
or later in the confessional
or at times to walk
close to windows,
along the nearest image of myself,
away from the curb, the falling
off into any hole,
the complete loss of limbs,
and to hope each day for growth,
regeneration, depending upon
the exercise of a hand-
shake or salute
and always with my right hand
to sign the cross
or X in the space provided.

Again all things considered,
please be seated,
smoking is permitted to the left,
never in the aisle,
on the right, I repeat the oath,
we grow where God plants us.

Her Fourth Ph.D. Discuss Party

The plate hangs heavy on her fingers,
a strain on her loss of spoons
in conversation, a silence at her knees
where the men sit, itching

China, a point to be made
on Pound—this aging nymph
in the back room, proving oral delivery
the test of stamina

for the mind, for the etymology
of sounds on the upper lip,
a concentration surviving thoughts of meat
balls and shrimp. She is limp

in body, at the knees, her plate
a kneeling bed. She has prayed ahead
for strength to pass this test,
this long toss of the word "Moloch!"

across each skull, each ball
a brain to pick, each itch
a foreign tongue to the men who rule contra-diction,
"short of the mark, the next time she'll pass
hors d'oeuvres."

Underground Wine Cellar, Athens, Greece

The old faces, losing teeth,
are staring deeper into wine
these days in their underground patch
of barley barrels, crates of pine logs,
checkered cloth and round tables, staring
down their noses through mugs of *robola*.
Again the revelation, a figure staggering, the nose
man near the nostrils issuing decrees.
Their eyes attend obedience school.
They tug in opposite directions, two dogs, on cue
walking a drunkard on a leash.

Silence in their thirst,
they would like to touch each other
to prove their senses work,
to hear their fingers give a speech
on servitude: *Greek noses are never what they
      seem.*
But no one moves or speaks,
staring down that glass of wine
like a goatherder down a cliff-side
from the high places in his mind.

Lately they regret possessions.
They have saved the gold capped in their teeth.
They fear the nose man,
crouching on the bridge
like a thief watching through the irons,

the endless motions of their tongues,
as if he translates one missed sip as language,
grounds for impasse, sedition,
a call for joining arms.

They will sit for days, weighted down
like empty vats, fat with ass-skin,
soaking up the final drops, thinking safe
eyes age like old wines,
better stored in barrels, underground.
At times an eye will blink to relieve itself
or reminisce of Parthenons and ageless caryatids.
But the iris fears its self-reflection,
its progeny, a drunkard straddling the nose,
frothing, snarling on his knees
at old dogs with lineage, Spartan pedigrees,
gold capped in their teeth.

Backward Years

I

These are backward years.
Dogs are not always dogs
or what they seem
to drunks or graveyard walls
who, merged in sleep, pose for leaks
or slow whimpers of midnight's passed wind.
Dogs, like grave diggers, hunt bones for reunions.

And whales are not always whales
or what they seem
to fish or fishermen,
who riding the tooth of a Jonah jaw
are spewed aground
like hunks of meat, beached rot-backs,
spawning worms with instinct.
Whales, like worms, control the spot they breed.

II

We over-estimate our powers
of memory, the mind's dark tree,
hatchet, wind, stump, the swift slice
of a brain cut to size.
We leave such little proof of ourselves.

Unless by taming dogs
or whales, sonars of intelligence,
we can teach the weight of rumps and knees
and riders,
cocked like triggers, teaching death.

We thrive on amnesia—
forgetting men, like presidents and kings,
are only men
no matter what they seem
to all themselves or privately.
Even gods lose their minds
like children's toys
and are misplaced as simply
and as often
as they seem to matter.

IV

IN THE TALKING HOURS

*and good when we are forgotten—
the design of death.*

Djuna Barnes
Nightwood

In the Talking Hours

1

In the talking hours we cannibals,
spoon salt out of gills
to preserve our flesh, stiff with the blood of a whale,
stripped to its bowels.

The light from a fire dies out.
My girl whispers behind the doors
to breathe in, to fall
back into the stroke and again the same pull
of oars against kelp. Her same whole
body rows without fault
imagining escape
through miles of lolled cod hacked clean.
        Amon, the fisherman, calls.
We must gut the fish, their entrails
steaming in his throat. Outside a gull circles
down to pick the scraps, crawls
in, wings matted by fishbone, now settles
near the whale, his hulk shelled like sandcrystals.
At night I wear scales around my skull.

2

In winter we build totems
out of driftwood and walk the mound
smooth, hands and knees, until we sleep
alone where the ocean skins the corners of the
 boathouse.
Ruined dogs bark waves on the run;
they teeth our flesh brown.
Their tongues drip with the juice of backbones.

Even out of dreams we count
our body wounds, the deep blood, how the veins
suck air into their sponge.
We breathe fish odors, whale dung,
and watch how even mullets eat their young
and beds we climb for leisure sound
spooked by love-groans.
 It is spawn season.
The air suffocates with flesh. It is the last month
of talking words still our own,
and we celebrate with lovemaking, nearly out of skin,
locking thighs in tune with radios. Soon
the fishmarkets close. The flesh gone bone
rattles in the open bins
like kettle drums.

Bringing a Stark Reality to the Screen

to Ingmar Bergman

The second feature,
and our eyes bounce off our salty hands,
frozen for the moment, popcorn
near our tongues.

The corpse is washed ashore.
Seaweed spills from its mouth.
The fisherman hooks his anchor to the catch
and hops it to the net.
This is not quite what we expected.

Of course we know the lesson
to be learned: how to victim
somewhere loses will to stay afloat.
But what drove our hero, hands tied, to the depth
where treading feet to break his fall,
he snatched the jewels between his teeth
                            and sinking
lodged them safely in his throat?

After intermission we will see the pearls
carved out of his testicles
           and wonder
at his wonder
when the fisherman casts him back as bait.

Dead Black Judy

victim of the KKK, Pittsburgh, 1970

1 *Offertory*

Black limbs bursting out of wild light,
rents of blood tossed like paint
along the shadows of your running,
you trip curbs that jump to meet you,
lamps that lean into your mind
like needles edging closer to the vein
or rain falling red above the siren's humming.
The dog's stale breath
licks your nose with sweat.
The sidewalk sprawls you like a trashcan
coughing up its foam into a dog's howl,
hungry for the flesh and not the bone.

2 *Transubstantiation*

You begin again to rise from your pose,
to exercise in walking like a paralytic,
bending in your drab, dark corner
to touch your toes, to hear the silence
breathe into your form
until the one clear song of bullets
lifts you like conjecture
out of the rumor of your name.
In their pistol scheme,
they shot yo«r body through
with rivets, sand, and butts
and called it architecture.

3 *Elevation*

They intone by moonlight, sons of fire,
who celebrate your body's host,
blood and wine, toast of hooded monks
leading the entourage of saints, masked,
around the midnight cross.
They toss each phallic torch
and crouch on fours
to nail drunk whores to beds.
They drink the flame's intoxication.
Down at Harley's Mother John
sings Rigoletto with a bosom ache;
Father Blanche breaks his mouth's bottle
on a toilet bowl flushing through falsetto.

4 *Communion*

You are dead, black Judy.
Your gangrene stare twists among the eyes
that click you into permanence,
bulbs exploding to amputate
the blackness of your vision,
to bury you in angles, lines, and proofs
of negatives fading white
where black had all your face.
You ran to the sun's mirror
knowing that Icarian flights
end sadly in the sea where they buried God,
that the flashing multi-universal lights
burn your mind's debris.

Moon Cows and Cow Tails

for an autistic child in the foster home

1

Say good-bye no more, Neil Tracy,
to the sand-dance of cars along the side-walk road,
or the balloon-bird bobbing bat-toes in your tub,

to the pantomime of moon-cows
swimming in the green boat. They need love.
Squeeze their udders to make them fly.

Those sails are wings, the cow-tails
rudders you steer to get them into sky.
Jump them over the broom-tree, over the rag-cloud,

then dive them back into the tub, back into the bow.
Plastics never swallow water. They are made to
       float,
but moon-cows sink of thirst. They are made of
       earth.

2

You are going home, Neil Tracy.
Tease your shadow. Dance it in the sun.
Jump it like a rope until it jumps back into you.

Be your own earth, your own face. Say good-bye no more
to the clay-face mould turning big-nose to your thumbs.
Shape it one last time, a moon-cow dreaming clothes,

and dream how cautiously you grow,
incubating in your skein of bones, your fragile limbs.
You need love like all things, inviolate, displaced.

Lombardo at Midnight, New Years Eve, 1972

for the Vietnam MIA's

It was neither the fire we trimmed
like hair, thick and full
of body, nor the wood

we cut for fuel out of spruce—
that warmed us, took us back
to you, back to our roots. Their use

came later during crow
fights on the ledge where we planted
bread and watched the new

year falling like a beak
on pale snow. We wanted memories
of the moon hitting ground,

a crowd to count it down,
to seconds, to the moment
of impact, some new force

pulling on our blood, a rose
growing out of flesh,
out of season with its seed. We needed

rhythm, a new song for the birth
of Eve. We wanted that and more,
a story for the song we called *ennui*.

Instead you gave us back
the bricks and mortar, our beds to lie in,
forefathers in sleep, tracking down the alien

creed—Live and let die, for peace sake—
our heroes, nametags on their genitals.
You gave us back their schedule,

crucifixion by time-clock, your woodwinds
blowing the same red ball off its edge
ike a man falling head-first into earth.

Just that Moment

> *Sgt. Dwight Johnson, 23, died today after he was shot four times by the owner of a store police say he was trying to rob. Johnson was cited for valor four years earlier by President Johnson who bestowed the Congressional Medal of Honor Nov. 19, 1968.* (AP)

1

Just that moment
before you lost
your mind
and fought through
scraps of hand
grenades and flesh,
hesitating

in the clutch,
hand to hand,
each wound becoming
face, and face
the metal of a gun,
you felt the first

prick deep inside your eyes
and knew the black-
out of pain
within the smiles dead heroes wear,
ribbon-white,
like medals on their chests.

2

That day you won
the honor,
there were other signs of rotting,
another wound inside the skull:
your own face
hesitating

to become the smile your leader smiled.
What charmed you? Survival—
or the death you owed
for being flesh
and twice alive

or metal,
the sound of it
against the clerk's skull
in that storeroom
just before the gun reared
and flashed
its slug into your blood.

You wanted permanence,
a chance to heal
flesh and mind.
You no longer heard
the cold
blood of metal
sapping at your lips
nor the coins
spinning on the counter
hesitating to be still
until they fell
and rolled that solid beat of drums.

Umbrella Man of Duquesne

He no longer walks his sack,
hands wet along the bench where he slept
with late news and hunched back.
His hat, the odor of bird stains.

His clothes fit any season,
hand-outs like his umbrellas,
patched with oil cloth and grease

to keep the rain out,
to keep the smell of living
ong his business at each door
where he pined the hard-sale,
his art of spinning parasols,
of blowing up the ribs
without a hitch or leak.

To widows, by Grace, his fifth wife,
he swore to be a virgin. Umbrella Man
of a dying breed, his handle
balls were pure antiques
and well preserved like saddle hide
in soap or ambergris.

Tonight at Mercy's Cancer Ward
he prays with double back a single vision—
the raining in his joints to leave
for a last-chance nurse
who once, for a dime, he bartered
the seduction of her middle class
with hosiery
and rubbers for her feet.

Huckster at Noontime

For Ján Palach, Czechoslovakia, 1968

1

In Humenne, in this time of drought,
when the sun and sky
caress like undulating forms,
slow to love in their callow way,

where poets
with fragile appetites and all-day dreaming
twist their spines through jive-talk parlors
like insects through a hammock,

I think of the chrysalis,
how the moth smothers in a spreading flame,
wings itself to death,
too early for the wind.

And I think of the Huckster,
black as *Tatra* rock,
his ring-boned haridelles, blinders cocked,
down at Market Square,
crates of fruit dying early in their season.

2

One day in six,
the red rose wilts in his lapel,
the jewels turn to glass on his thumbs,
his wheel rims, rolling free-fall in tall air,
stick fast to the customers,
ringing bells
like wards of maternity

for the Mother-load,
for the ripe milk of melons,
souring like the odor of hoofs and tails.
They have no schedule,
these umbilicates,
exiled in the sleep of their conception.

They save religion for the Friday sale,
for the revolutionary,
their *kamelot*,
thief with stolen horses,
huckstering fruit
like news on the anniversary of death.
True patriots are shot for less.
RIPE FRUIT FOR GOLD, headlines
on the foot-boards, on the tailgate,
CREDIT WITH ROSARIES TO HOLD.
No one suspects his alchemy.

Celebrant of the extreme
unction, patron of the healing arts,
he spits into nicks of melon bellies,
grinds the sap, the worms,
the spittle of tobacco shreds.
Even corn whiskey turns to gold on his breath.

    3

I think of the stench,
the rotted fruit, the cankered skin
like wizened breasts of nuns,
how the juice once flowed,
flesh splitting, wet as lips.

And now his treason,
this aching flesh of worms,
blotting the tongue white,
transparent as onions,
the veins like delicate moth wings.

He plays the martyr, liberator,
the huckster out of season,
dropping apple-cores
where now the children lie,
picking roots of rampion
out of the cobblestones of *Svermova*.
Bodies back at Wenceslaus
rot red beneath the statue's sword.

To Pregnancy

a toast by Yevgeny Yevtushenko

I

You call me brother,
embrace me like the warm belly
of a wife. Sounds of kicking in your ear,
on your tongue, this word, its knife
cutting wounds into a poem
to free the blood, to fill its body
with a first-born. In wounds
you learn the freedom of birth.
You give your sons their names.

We would have grown up
in *Zima* where the pines fall barefoot
on still water. At night, shallow graves.
Everything sleeps near the lake.
The walk takes breath. In a step
we might have drowned
all our limbs to fill the lungs in our heads.

In *Cernina* we might have crawled
the length of an oak to sleep
where the moon knots an eye in the bark.
Always in the first dark of sleep,
we dream we are immortal.

But we have learned our boundaries,
to fall with an oak, headfirst
through its own space of light, out of vision,
like a tooth, or an axe
to hear the shock, the split
second dark
of silence in our cracked skulls.

II

This is backward talk.
Poets, inheritors at birth, we grow absent,
minded by our years like rotted apples
or vacant fields seeking the graves of trees.
We are weaned to death
with losses, extinction, with breasts,
searching for a woman,
as if the world in the round of her lake
were feeding us breath. She alone
knows the ache in our lungs,
where the sea goes to drown its limbs,
what the oak dreams, fallen bird
spreading limbs to remember the flight.

V

THE SINGING HOUR

Teach us to kill humanely.
John Lennon

Junky Saints

An Elegy for Valerie Swan (1948-1970)

1

Those junky saints slept near you,
dreaming you in time,
breathing you in the faint
lines of bedsheets, in love with flesh,
in love with breath;
          all your ancestors bawling

in the dark room, in that howling bed,
dog-screams of head
shaking out its needle-point,
its fluid from the brain,
coughs that never stopped you
short of rain-walks,
              short
of easing past the same
soft whisper of your corner saints,
fixing all the world's hinges,
all the doors swinging out
into dreams of father, husband, lover,
out o touch
        and touching you too late.

2

All night you heard their steps,
the wind-sweep of voices
where your cousin lay dressed
white in the dark of cameras,
her face shuttered like an opened lens.
          You buried her
a thousand times in cardboard walls
of yellow boxes, in the home
wood of floors you walked
to still the humming in your flesh.
               Their voices, dream-still,
repeated themselves like stairs to the second floor—
UGANGA, SHAUKU, UGANGA—
shaping silence of an image
near your bed. Still no sign
of father
          in the needle's throat;
only dogs howling, rain howling,
all your ancestors bawling
in the dark room, in the yellow
box without hinges, bed without hinges,
doors swinging out.

3

Your cousin dreams you now
inside your burning car—
artist, hairdresser, manicurist
of hands singed by the metal's flesh,
your coat's burned sleeve still breathes
that touch of fire
                in your veins,
in your eyes each time you gessoed canvas space
or rearrangeu the color tones to balance frames,
remembering how it was to be still
born, to create infinitely
your own body's breath,
                      igniting spirit
like the rush of fingers
through hair you shaped to resurrect a face;
all the faces, cracked by mirrors
or stain-glassed doors.
                      You sang your fire song
in the chorus touch of church hands,
in the rimes of ash, the broken glass of wind
songs on the street with sleepers, walkers,
cab drivers, drunk with speed
to arrive where leaving begins.

4

And leaving, your voice remains
a half-memory for junky saints.
      Lovers, starved by fire,
their breath could find no wind
or rain to swallow, no tongues to touch.
They have known the bone bottoms of the mind,
the breaking out and shaking in;
their own bodies' dying habit
of the flesh
     inhaling
one last breath of you,
one last song until their bones heal
and their bodies root to mound your field,
each needle-point its own flower,
each limb its own hinge
       to lock you in
where the dead pass hours like low wind,
like saints howling, children howling,
all your ancestors bawling
in the dark room, in the coffin
frame without hinges, bed without hinges,
doors swinging in.

5

We survive the walk down slope,
threaded images of mound and sight-
seers trimming grass for snow.
Our voices scream out before us
into the sudden cold of crypts
we build for steps
                    into earth,
into the roots of your bones, the almost grown
vision of ourselves, all fathering,
loving, sharing one flesh, one touch of you
to survive ourselves, to heal
our bodies in,
                    to remain
here in this world of hinges
where so much depends upon face
becoming the image of a sun,
where there are no suns, no fire
in the veins of this sky,
no infinite creation of the single breath
or the last breath
                    singing

cures to our tongues
until we become the faces
of the blind you resurrect, half-deaf
to your voice becoming song,
ur ancestor singing in the still room, waking
us to wind, to the touch of fire
moving back into our minds,
into our breath
         and touching us in time.

Presented at Heinz Chapel, University of Pittsburgh for the Valerie Swan Foundation, Pittsburgh, Pa.

November 28, 1972

About the Author

James Ragan is an internationally recognized poet and has lived in Prague, Paris, Athens, and Beijing. He has been honored here and abroad as an ambassador of poetry. In 1985 he was one of three Americans, including Robert Bly and Bob Dylan, invited to perform for Mikhail Gorbachev at the First International Poetry Festival in Moscow. He has since performed for five international heads of state including Czech President Vaclav Havel. Other venues have included Tokyo, Hong Kong, London, Sofia, Vienna, Paris, Warsaw, Prague, and New York, where he performed twice at Carnegie Hall and at the United Nations. He is the recipient of numerous poetry honors including two Fulbright Professorships (Yugoslavia and China), the Emerson Poetry Prize, eight Pushcart Prize nominations, an NEA, a Presidential Medal (St. Vincent College), and a Poetry Society of America Gertrude Claytor award. He is the author of *In the Talking Hours, Womb-Weary, The Hunger Wall, Lusions, The World Shouldering I,* and *Too Long a Solitude,* and the plays *The Landlord, Saints,* and *Commedia* (first produced by Raymond Burr in the U. S. and later the Soviet Union). He also co-edited *Yevgeny Yevtushenko, Collected Poems: 1952–1990.* His poetry has been recorded on Sony/Alfa Records and on *A Century of Recorded Poetry* for Rhino Records. He has a Ph.D. and is the director of the Graduate Professional Writing Program at the University of Southern California. In 1996 Buzz Magazine named him "one of the 100 coolest people in Los Angeles: those who make a difference."

Acknowledgements

Acknowledgement is extended to the following publications in which these poems originally appeared: *Bachy, Back Door, Bitterroot, Blackbird Circle, Boxspring, Confrontation, Expression* (U.K.), *Greenfield Review, Intro #4, Jeopardy, The Little Magazine, Midwest Quarterly, Mundus Artium, Northwest Review, Poetry Northwest, Road Apple Review, Southern Poetry Review, Trace, West Coast Poetry Review,* and *The University of Windsor Review.* "Losing a Sense of Balance" was originally published in *The Ohio Review.* "Delivering My Brother, the Last Born," copyright © 1973 by Washington and Lee University is reprinted from *Shenandoah: The Washington and Lee University Review* with the permission of the editor.